Footprints of Faith:
The Changemakers

Footprints of Faith:
The Changemakers

Nancy Walbank

Illustrated by Maxine Lee-Mackie

First published in Great Britain in 2025 by Hodder & Stoughton
An Hachette UK Company

1

Copyright © Nancy Walbank 2025
Illustrations copyright © Maxine Lee-Mackie 2025

The right of Nancy Walbank to be identified as the Author of the Work has been asserted by her in accordance with the Copyright, Designs and Patents Act 1988.

All rights reserved. No part of this publication may be reproduced, stored in a retrieval system, or transmitted, in any form or by any means without the prior written permission of the publisher, nor be otherwise circulated in any form of binding or cover other than that in which it is published and without a similar condition being imposed on the subsequent purchaser.

A CIP catalogue record for this title is available from the British Library

Trade Paperback ISBN 978 1 399 81809 4
ebook ISBN 978 1 399 8181 0

Typeset in Sabon MT by Hewer Text UK Ltd, Edinburgh
Printed and bound in Great Britain by Clays Ltd, Elcograf S.p.A.

Hodder & Stoughton policy is to use papers that are natural, renewable and recyclable products and made from wood grown in sustainable forests. The logging and manufacturing processes are expected to conform to the environmental regulations of the country of origin.

Hodder & Stoughton Ltd
Carmelite House
50 Victoria Embankment
London EC4Y 0DZ

www.hodderfaith.com

John Murray Press, part of Hodder & Stoughton Limited
An Hachette UK company

The authorised representative in the EEA is Hachette Ireland, 8 Castlecourt Centre, Dublin 15, D15 XTP3, Ireland (email: info@hbgi.ie)

Introduction

What stories from childhood are still in your head? When I take a moment to think about this, pictures come to mind from books read to me, along with the sound of the long-gone storyteller's voice. I remember a box of Bible stories for children that arrived at our house from a jumble sale. I poured over the pictures before I could read the words but soon learned about Jesus, the helper, and the stories he told. Stories matter because they communicate with us as information and as characters and places that come alive in our imaginations, leaving their mark and helping us shape a sense of who we are whether or not we realise this.

In writing this book, I wanted children to experience stories from scripture and stories about Christians who have led remarkable lives in a way that resonates with them and sparks their curiosity. For this reason, all the stories in this collection involve contemporary children stepping back through time to hear a story about a person or an event and, through the characters of modern children, asking questions. In doing this, children encounter a story in a modern worldview, ask questions about it, and then form a personal response through a short activity at the end of each story. In RE lessons, the stories will help orient children into the time of Jesus, for example, by thinking how difficult it is to make a hole in someone's roof before encountering the scriptural text. When learning about saints, children will learn about the time in history the saint lived in, think about the changes that happened because of their faith and how these changes resonate with people today. Each story is a glimpse into a life or an event, a first step in learning and an invitation to follow the footprints of faith.

I hope you enjoy reading it and sharing it with others. It may spark an interest in the history of a place or person and the changes that happened as a result of their choices or change your thoughts about a familiar story from scripture as you follow the golden footprints through time.

Nancy Walbank

Contents

1	Joan the Maid	*Joan of Arc*	1
2	Hild the Peacemaker	*Hild of Whitby*	15
3	The Cave at Greecio	*Francis of Assisi*	27
4	Lucky Josephine	*Josephine Bakhita*	39
5	Saint of the Broom	*Martin de Porres*	53
6	Blessed are the Poor?	*Matthew 5:1–11*	67
7	The Centurion's Servant	*Luke 7:1–10*	81
8	The Hole in the Roof	*Luke 5:17–26*	93
9	The forgiving father	*Luke 15:11–32*	107
10	Tongues of Fire	*Acts 2:1–13*	119

1
Joan the Maid
Joan of Arc

'I'm sure that it is a girl,' said Mart, gazing at the picture on the art gallery's wall.

'It can't be,' Luiz replied. 'Girls don't wear armour.'

Mart stared at the figure in the painting, who wore a suit of armour but also looked too young to be a knight. The label next to the painting said, 'Saint Joan of Arc', but saints said prayers and helped people. They didn't wear suits of armour. She ran her fingers through her short, brown hair and looked down at her T-shirt and jeans, imagining putting on heavy armour like the person in the painting and riding into a battle.

'I think anyone can wear armour if they want, Luiz. I think I would.'

Luiz pulled a face at his sister. 'Come on, let's go and find a gallery guide to help us.'

The children walked away, looking for an explanation of the mysterious person in the painting.

'Look, Luiz.' Mart pointed to some golden footprints on the floor. 'Maybe they will lead us to a guide?'

Following the footprints, the children found an archway covered by a dark red curtain edged with gold fabric.

'Oh, how fancy!' Mart said as she pulled back the curtain.

They walked into what seemed to be a huge tent, bustling with people.

'Is this a living museum bit? It smells funny, a bit like horse poo!' Luiz pinched his nose as they looked around.

Mart resisted the urge to pinch her nose like Luiz. There was a strong, sweaty smell of farm animals, but she could only see people inside the big brown tent, busily placing wooden bowls and food on a brown table that stretched down the middle.

'Why are you two just standing there? There is so much work to do before the coronation!'

Mart and Luiz turned towards the speaker, who stared at them, hands on her hips and head to one side. She wore a long, grey dress with white sleeves, an apron around her waist and a white scarf tied around her head.

'Pardon us,' Mart answered. 'We are a bit lost. We were looking for some information about Joan of Arc because we didn't understand the painting we were looking at.'

'Joan of Arc?' The lady pulled a face. 'I don't know a Joan of Arc. Do you mean Joan the Maid? Her father is called Jacques d'Arc, but it's not her name. Everyone calls her the Maid because she is so young.'

'Does she sometimes wear armour? Like a knight?'

'Of course! Have you been sleeping under a rock not to know about Joan, or are you English spies?' The lady glared at them.

Thinking how to answer very quickly before they were taken for spies, Luiz replied, 'My name is Luiz, named after my father who is from Portugal, and this is my sister, Mart.'

'I'm Charlotte.' The lady pointed at herself. 'Portugal is far from France, is it not? Perhaps that is why you do not know about the Maid and why you are wearing strange clothes.'

Mart and Luiz nodded in agreement.

'Help me to scrub the carrots for the coronation feast and I will share what I know about Joan.'

Agreeing, Luiz and Mart followed Charlotte into the kitchen where a mountain of dirty vegetables sat. As they sat on stools and received scrubbing brushes from Charlotte, Mart realised that the carrots were all different colours – purple, white and yellow, but not the familiar orange of home. Picking up a carrot each, they all started scrubbing as Charlotte told her story.

'Of course, you know that the English have been fighting the French for many, many years – what feels like forever. They believe the country belongs to them, and lots of battles have happened over the last hundred years. Well, Joan first appeared when it seemed that the English were winning. She wanted to speak to Charles, the dauphin, a prince of France and leader of the army, who was holding a council at the great castle of Chinon in the Loire Valley. Some called it the council of despair! Joan appeared with six knights, saying she had a message from God. At first, she was mistaken for a boy as she wore a tunic and breeches, not a dress, and under her black, woollen cap, her hair was cropped as short as yours.' Charlotte pointed to Mart.

'But who was she? Where did she come from?' Luiz asked.

'I am coming to that!' sighed Charlotte, picking another carrot from the pile. 'Of course, you can't just turn up and speak to the dauphin saying you've heard a message from God. You might be making it up!

'Joan's family are simple farmers. She said she had heard the voice of an angel when she was only thirteen. No one believed her, and her father decided she should get married as soon as possible to stop her nonsense. But Joan said her life belonged to God, so when she was sixteen, she convinced the local judge that she should not be forced to marry the man her father chose. You see, this was already extraordinary. As a girl, Joan was her father's property. But she knew God had a deeper purpose for her life.

'Joan heard an angel give her a message for Charles, and him alone. So, Joan travelled to find him even though she was only sixteen and knowing how dangerous the war made travelling.

'When Joan first arrived among Charles's supporters, she found he was away in a distant castle. She spoke to Robert de Baudricourt, an army captain. At first, he did not believe a young girl. Yet, Joan spoke so passionately about God's message to drive away the English, that many of Charles's supporters began to think that she was the one who would save France from them. Robert gave her an escort of six knights and took her to see Charles the dauphin. Thinking like a soldier, Joan cut her hair short and wore men's clothes for the journey to the castle where Charles was holding his council.'

'I remember, you said they despaired because there was no hope for the French,' Mart interrupted. Wondering about the painting they had seen, she continued, 'What did they say about her wearing men's clothes? Did the king give her a suit of armour?'

Charlotte paused as a young boy pushed past her carrying a huge basket full of delicious smelling bread.

'Keep listening and scrubbing, please.' Charlotte pointed at Mart's empty hands. 'Charles agreed to speak to Joan, he had nothing to lose, and she told him God's angel had promised her she would see him crowned king. She asked him for an army to lead to Orléans, a northern city that was surrounded by the English. Charles knew there was something special about our Joan. Against the advice of his generals, Charles sent Joan into battle wearing a white suit of armour, riding a white horse to fight the English army at Orléans. Joan wrote a letter to the English, telling them to hand over the city's keys to her, the Maid. If they did not, she would make them leave. She was coming on behalf of the King of Heaven to send the English back to their land! When they did not move, Joan led the French army against the English again and again until the English were forced to retreat. Orléans was free!'

'So have the English returned to England?' Luiz asked, picking one of the last carrots off the pile.

'Not yet, but they have drawn back, so today we are crowning Charles as the true French king here in Reims, and Joan the Maid will be at his side, just as she said.'

'Charlotte!' a voice called. 'Where are the vegetables?'

'Oh my! I must help prepare the feast!' Charlotte scooped up the basket of scrubbed carrots. As she left the tent, she turned, saying, 'Go towards the cathedral and you might see the Maid. She is only sixteen, and yet, she has saved France!'

'Shall we go?' Mart asked Luiz.

'Perhaps if we follow the footprints again, we will find our way to the Maid?' Luiz pointed to where footprints marked the floor.

Mart nodded her agreement, and they stepped out of the tent back into the art gallery.

'Oh! What just happened?' Luiz asked.

'I don't know,' replied Mart, 'but there are still footprints to follow, maybe we can find out?'

Following the footprints, they found themselves in front of a different painting. It showed a young woman dressed in armour, lit by a puddle of sunlight, in the middle of what looked like a church full of men. All the men looked angry. Some were pointing at the girl, some were writing things down, and one wore the pointed hat of a bishop.

'What's this painting about? Is that Joan the Maid?' asked Luiz.

A lady was also looking at the painting. She turned to face Luiz, who saw she was wearing a badge that read 'Hello, I'm Enu, museum guide' pinned to her blue shirt.

'It's interesting that you are not calling her Joan of Arc.'

'Well, we met someone who said Arc was her father's name, and who told us how Joan led the French to victory and was with Charles when he was crowned king,' Mart explained.

The lady smiled a sad smile. 'But things didn't turn out too well for Joan after that. Do you want to hear the end of the story?'

Mart and Luiz nodded.

'Well, after her fantastic victory at Orléans, Joan's reputation as a leader spread far and wide and she escorted Charles across enemy territory to Reims, where he was crowned in 1429.

'Joan believed the French should fight to retake Paris. Unfortunately, some of Charles's advisers were jealous of how powerful Joan had become and they encouraged him to question her advice. So, the English had time to regroup with support from a French nobleman, the Duke of Burgundy. When Joan attacked Paris, the English army was stronger, and she lost the battle. Charles then ordered Joan to confront an enemy attack on Compiègne. She was thrown from her horse and captured by the Duke of Burgundy's followers, who took her to the English.'

'Oh no!' Mart gasped. 'What did they do to her?'

'Nothing good.' Enu shook her head sadly. 'This painting shows how they put her on trial, accusing her of many things, including being a witch, making up her story about receiving messages from God, which was called heresy, and dressing like a man.'

'Wow! Dressing how she chose was a crime?' asked Luiz.

'It was considered improper behaviour for a woman,' Enu explained. 'After a long trial and imprisonment, Joan signed a confession. However, she defiantly dressed in male clothing when they pronounced her guilty and condemned her to be burned as a witch and heretic. Charles did not help her, and Joan was burned at the stake in 1431. She was only nineteen.'

They all stood silently for a moment, looking at the painting. A tear crept down Luiz's cheek.

'Her story can't end like that! She was amazing and brave.' Mart's words were choked in a sob.

'Well, her story is still being told today. Look at the paintings we have.' Enu pointed around the room. 'She changed what was happening in the war, meaning Charles finally defeated the English in 1453. Then, he ordered a new trial, and Joan was found innocent of all the charges. People have written books about Joan and made films about her. In 1920, she was declared a saint and is now the patron saint of France. Her story is still changing people's lives.'

Mart took her brother's hand and squeezed it tightly.

'We will tell your story, Joan,' she promised.

Joan (1412–1431) grew up on her parents' farm in northeast France. France was engaged in a long-standing war with the invading English. The English kings believed they were the rightful heirs to the French crown and had been at war with France since 1337, seventy-five years before Joan was born.

Joan began having visions around the age of thirteen, which convinced her that God was guiding her to become a soldier. Her victories against the aggressive English army were a turning point in the war as the French reclaimed significant cities, such as Orléans and Reims, from the English. Joan cut across age and gender roles and gained recognition as the saviour of France. Her faith in God's purpose for her life changed the events of the war and France's future. On 16 May 1920, she was declared a saint by the Roman Catholic Church. Joan is known by many names, including Joan of Arc and the Maid of Orléans.

> Can you create a motto that sums up Joan's life and mission?

2
Hild the Peacemaker
Hild of Whitby

'We have to go all the way up there!' Ollie pointed at the stone steps that climbed steeply upwards. 'I can't see what's at the top!'

'Race you!' called Alexander, three steps ahead of his brother.

'Be careful, boys! There are 199 steps, and people might be coming down!' shouted Mum at her children's disappearing backs.

Alexander stopped by a bench, gasping for breath. Ollie collapsed onto the seat.

'Ollie, last one there buys the ice creams?' Alexander set off again.

'That will be Mum!' Ollie huffed to his feet and tramped up the steps.

Alexander sat on the top step, watching the gulls flying high in the sky, and looked out across the town of Whitby to the sea.

Ollie sat beside him.

'I'm tired, there's no ice cream van and nothing to do except look at another ruined building. Why does Mum make us do educational stuff?' he complained.

'You could watch the birds. See how they dip their wings as they fly over the ruin?' Alexander suggested.

'That sounds boring!' said Ollie. 'I'm going to follow those footprints and see where they go.'

Alexander hadn't seen the golden footprints leading away from the top of the steps towards the ruin that looked like an old church, with stone arches pointing to the sky. Not wanting to lose his brother, he followed.

'Ollie, wait!' Alexander called, following the footprints around a bend and almost bumping into his brother.

'They lead to that stone cross,' said Ollie. 'Race you!'

As they arrived at the stone cross, a tall man with a big smile greeted them.

'Good day to you both. Are you here to see the Mother?'

The boys were surprised to see that he was wearing a long robe that might have once been white, tied with a rope around the waist.

'Our mother is still coming up the steps. Who are you, please?' asked Alexander, wondering if they should talk to this man. He looked older than Mum, with white hair and a crinkled face. Alexander rummaged in his head for the word to describe him and his clothes. He was a monk!

'I meant, have you come to see Mother Hild?' the man replied. 'I am Cædmon, I look after the cows, but you find me trying to remember a poem that came to me in a dream last night.'

Before the man could start reciting poetry, Ollie asked, 'Is Hild the name of your mother? She must be very old.'

Cædmon laughed. 'No and yes. She is the mother of everyone living in this community. Where have you travelled from that you do not know Hild?'

'We are here for the Easter holidays,' Ollie replied. 'Mum said it would be educational.'

'Your mother is right. Many people come here to learn from Hild, and she is an expert on Easter. Sit, and eat with me while I tell you about her story.'

Alexander and Ollie sat on the grass as Cædmon dipped bowls into a wooden bucket.

'Enjoy milk from my cows and a taste of honeyed oatcake and I will begin.'

'Hild's uncle Edwin was king of the great northern kingdom of Northumbria. She grew up in his castle overlooking the vast North Sea as a princess. She spent her days learning to manage a large kingdom and heard tales of famous battles from the warriors who served her uncle. Edwin followed the old ways and the old gods. But the light of Christ was travelling across the country. Edwin's wife was a follower of Christ. Edwin's family, including Hild, heard the teaching of Christ and were baptised by the Christian bishop Paulinus at York on Easter Sunday. For almost twenty years, Hild lived happily with her aunt and uncle until Edwin was killed in a battle with Penda, the King of Mercia. Hild feared for her life.'

Alexander stopped drinking his bowl of creamy milk. 'How scary! Did she escape to here?' he asked.

'Not yet,' Cædmon smiled. 'The bishop Paulinus helped Hild and her aunt escape to family in Kent. Hild was thirty-three and had spent her life as a princess. Confused, she wondered what to do next and decided God was calling her to him. She sought out Aidan of Lindisfarne. Perhaps you have heard of Lindisfarne?'

The boys mumbled 'No' as they munched on the delicious, sweet oatcakes.

'Well, it is a monastery, like here. A place where Christian people come to give their life to God. I am getting ahead of myself! Where was I?'

'You were telling us about Aidan,' Alexander reminded him.

'Hild changed her life. She became a holy sister, a nun, promising her life to God. Aidan persuaded her to set up a community for others who also wanted to devote their lives to God.

'First, she gathered a group of people at Stag Island, in the north, and then she called people to live here by the sea. We soon formed a community of nuns, monks, teachers and students, living lives of prayer but weaving, farming and fishing too. We live simply in those small wooden buildings. Hild teaches everyone to share their belongings, and her years living as a princess mean she is a good listener and sorts out our problems. Now, kings, princes and bishops come to Whitby asking for her wisdom.'

'I think being a princess is more interesting,' Ollie said, putting down his now empty bowl. 'I'd prefer battles.'

'It is not so different. However, here, battles happen with words, not swords. If Hild had stayed a princess, she would have had to marry, or serve another uncle. Here, she is head of our community in her own right. Why, as we sit here, she is holding a meeting with bishops and important men and women to decide a great matter.

'A sort of battle of words is taking place about the date of Easter. Perhaps you already know because you are here about the Easter holy day?'

'Yes, Mum brought us here for Easter,' Alexander replied, licking the last bit of honey from his fingers.

Cædmon nodded his head. 'Is your mother a scholar joining the discussion?'

'She is a teacher,' Ollie replied, hoping Mum hadn't secretly brought them to a meeting. 'Can I have some more milk, please, while you tell us what the meeting is about?'

'Well,' Cædmon explained, refilling their bowls, 'here, in the north, we are guided in our Christian faith by the Irish Celtic tradition because they were the people who brought the light of Christ to our shores. In the south, they follow the teachings of Rome as the Pope sent Augustine and his companions to bring Christ's teachings to the Angles who live in the south-east of the country.

'The Celts celebrate Easter using one calendar, Rome uses another, which means they celebrate Easter a week later. And here we have a problem,' said Cædmon. 'The northern king, Oswiu, and his wife have fallen out! She follows Rome and celebrates Easter a week after her husband. Her ladies were fasting while the men sat feasting. It has caused quite an argument. So, Hild has invited Oswiu and many other Christians here to a council to decide if Christians in the north should follow Rome.'

'What do you think should happen, Cædmon?' Ollie asked him.

'I think that God will guide Hild. She is not afraid of change because she changed her life to serve God. Hild guides us all to find our gifts. She believes I am a poet, not a cowherd. She says God has given me a gift!' Cædmon laughed, shaking his head.

'Look,' he pointed at the sky. 'If you watch the birds as they fly overhead, they dip their wings. They are bowing to Hild.'

The brothers watched the gulls circle overhead.

'They do look like they are waving hello,' said Alexander, thinking back to when he was watching them on the top step, and his mind turned to Mum.

'Thank you, Cædmon, for the food and the story. We need to find our mum.'

'Yes, and I must get back to my poem. Mother Hild wants me to recite something after tonight's feast when the date of Easter will have been decided.' Cædmon looked worried.

'Perhaps the birds might help you with your poem?' Ollie suggested. 'They remind me of the birds on my old pillowcase – their white wings waving against the sky-blue fabric.'

Cædmon slowly smiled. 'Hmm, Heaven's fabric ... something of my dream is returning. Perhaps God sent you two to be my inspiration.'

He waved them goodbye, murmuring, '"Praise we the fashioner now of Heaven's fabric", I think that's it.'

'Race you back!' Ollie shouted as he sprinted towards the steps.

Running to catch his brother, Alexander noticed the footprints had disappeared.

Mum stood at the top of the steps, reading an information board. The children threw their arms around her.

'Please can we have an ice cream now?' begged Ollie.

'In a minute,' Mum replied. 'Don't you want to find out a bit about Whitby Abbey first?'

'Oh, I know loads!' Ollie said. 'It started with a clever lady called Hild, and there was a big meeting where they decided when Easter would happen, which is why we are on holiday!'

'Wow! Where did you learn all that?' asked Mum.

'From a monk called Cædmon. He said he writes poetry, and he told us all about Hild. But he doesn't live in this big stone building. The monks and nuns live very simply in small wooden huts,' Alexander explained.

'You must have read it somewhere, or perhaps someone is role-playing, sweetheart. Cædmon and Hild lived a long time ago. Look, one of his poems is here.' Mum pointed at the information board and read out,

Praise we the fashioner now of Heaven's fabric,
The majesty of his might and his mind's wisdom.

Ollie and Alexander looked at each other.

'No way!' Ollie gasped.

HILD THE PEACEMAKER

'You're a poet and you don't know it!' Alexander giggled, then asked, 'Mum, please can we have a good look round here? I want to find out how things changed here because of Hild.'

Mum smiled at him. 'That's a good plan, but maybe ice cream first?'

> Have you ever noticed how the dates of the Easter holidays can change each year, whereas Christmas is always on 25 December? Things were even more confusing at the time of Hild (sometimes called Hilda, 614–680). Christians who followed the Pope in Rome celebrated a week after Christians who followed the Celtic Church.
>
> Kings and Christian thinkers from across Britain gathered at Hild's abbey to agree on a formula for calculating the date of Easter. The meeting is known as the Synod of Whitby. At the Synod, everyone decided to follow the Roman formula for calculating the date of Easter Sunday, the day Christians

celebrate Jesus' resurrection from the dead and recognise the Pope as the leader of the Christian Church. Easter would be celebrated on the Sunday after the first full moon following the spring equinox, the time when the hours of daylight become more than the hours of darkness. We still use this formula today.

Hild brought people together who disagreed. Can you imagine the skills she used to help everyone reach an agreement?

Hild encouraged Cædmon to be a poet instead of a cowherd. His poem about creation is one of the earliest examples of English poetry. How might nature inspire you to write a poem?

3
The Cave at Greccio
Francis of Assisi

'I'm sure you will enjoy decorating the Christmas crib more than watching a film,' said Nan.

Fran looked at his sister, Ava, and pulled a face.

'But it's Christmas, Nan,' replied Ava. 'We want to watch this Santa film. Christmas is all about watching movies and . . .'

'Eating chocolate!' interrupted Fran.

'Well,' Nan sighed, 'perhaps today we could do something I want to do and go to church. You might even find you enjoy yourself.'

Ava opened her mouth to argue that she already knew lots about Christmas because they were putting on a nativity play at school, but Fran shook his head, saying, 'OK Nan, let's go!'

They wrapped themselves in their winter coats and long scarves and set off on the short walk to church.

Even though it was still afternoon, the December day was growing dark, and the frosty air prickled Ava's nose, making her shiver. Outside the church, Nan started talking to a white-haired man carrying a large holly branch. Fran and Ava blew into their hands and stamped their feet against the cold. Ava pointed to golden footprints on the ground that led away from the church entrance.

'Shall we see where these footprints take us?' she asked her brother, who nodded and placed his feet in the footprints, singing 'Jingle bells'.

As they rounded the corner, Fran almost bumped into a man leading a donkey by a long rope.

'That is a merry tune you are singing,' said the man. 'Has Francis sent you to help with his new idea?' Still holding the rope, the man pointed towards what looked like the entrance to a rocky cave where a man stood in a splash of light cast by candles on the ground.

'I don't remember seeing this behind Nan's church before. Do you think it's Santa's grotto?' Ava whispered to Fran as the man continued.

'I am Bernard, one of Francis's followers. Do you live near here?'

THE CAVE AT GRECCIO

'No, we are staying with our grandmother for Christmas,' Fran answered. 'I'm Francis too, but everyone calls me Fran. Why do you have a donkey?'

'It is part of Francis's idea. Walk with me and I will tell you. Young Francis, will you lead the donkey?'

Fran took the rope, and the donkey trotted beside him as Bernard began.

'As visitors, you may not know about Francis. When a young man, he became a soldier. Unfortunately, he was captured in battle and imprisoned. Sick and lonely, he wondered about what would make his life happy. He decided he had been putting his attention on the wrong things, like becoming a famous soldier. After his release from prison, he gradually gave up all his wealth to devote his life to God.

'He started by caring for sick people, then he rebuilt a small, ruined church. He led a simple life with no possessions or fancy clothes. I noticed that even though Francis now owned nothing, he was happy. I decided to change my life too and I gave away everything and joined him. I was not alone. Now, we are a community of hundreds who follow Francis in announcing the stories of Jesus to all creation. Once, Francis even preached to a flock of birds! He told them they should thank God, who clothed them in feathers and gave them wings and the sky. The birds perched as though they were listening to him and only flew away after he blessed them with his hands.'

'Is that true?' Ava asked.

Bernard shrugged. 'Francis has an extraordinary way with animals. He always treats them with kindness because they are all God's creatures. I believe he could get the birds to eat out of his hand if he wanted. You will see when you meet him.'

'Is he going to bless this donkey? Is that why you are taking it to him?' asked Fran.

THE CAVE AT GRECCIO

'Not exactly,' Bernard answered. 'Let me explain. Francis says we must always follow the teachings of our Lord Jesus and walk in his footprints. To better understand Jesus' life, Francis visited Bethlehem and told me about a church that stands in the place where Jesus was born. He says it is ancient and beautiful, but we must remember that Jesus was born in a stable, a poor babe, surrounded by animals. He wants to change the way we think about Jesus' birth, to reconnect with the story Saint Luke tells us in his Gospel.'

As Bernard finished his story, they arrived at the entrance to the cave where a group of people had gathered. The donkey gave a loud 'heehaw' and a man came over and scratched the donkey's head. He wore a simple brown robe and had a circular bald patch at the top of his head where he had shaved off his hair. He smiled and spoke in a gentle voice.

'Welcome, everyone, I am Francis. Today, I want us to do something that will help us relive the story of the baby who was born in Bethlehem. Instead of just listening, we will see with our eyes the poverty of Jesus' birth, smell the stable, touch the prickly straw of the animal's food box where his mother placed him.'

'That is why we have brought the donkey,' Bernard whispered. 'So we can remember the noises and smells of a stable. See, someone else has brought a cow.'

As Ava looked around, she saw two boys carrying lambs, another man leading a large brown cow, and a lady holding a tiny baby bundled in a blanket against the cold. The man called Francis took the baby from the lady, gently placing the child in a straw-filled wooden box.

'Come,' said Francis. 'Gather around the child in the manger and remember that in our Christian faith, God came to us as a tiny baby in a stable, needing love and care.'

'It's like being in a school nativity play,' Fran told Ava. 'Look, the boys with the lambs are shepherds, the lady with the baby is Mary, and the man standing next to her, the one with the long walking stick, is Joseph.'

'Do you think this is what it was really like?' Ava asked Bernard. 'I've never really thought about it before, it's just a story we hear each year.'

Bernard smiled. 'Well, we don't know if a cow or a donkey were in the stable, the Gospels do not say, but it helps us to imagine and to remember that baby Jesus had nothing, not even a place to sleep, so Mary placed him in a box that was for animal feed.'

THE CAVE AT GRECCIO

One of the lambs started to bleat, so Francis took it from the boy, wrapping it in the folds of his brown robe. As the lamb quietened, he spoke again.

'On this night, we are going to say Mass around the manger of hay and remember the Christ child.'

'Is that where Christmas comes from, Christ Mass?' Fran wondered.

Bernard laughed. 'What did you think Christmas was about?'

Fran and Ava looked at each other for a long moment.

'I think we should get Nan,' said Ava.

'Yes, let's tell her we've found the meaning of Christmas in this stable,' Fran replied.

Looking back at the scene one last time, Ava thought again how difficult it must have been for Mary. She was looking after a new baby with nothing to help her, and she thought about the smells and noises of the animals.

Shaking her head, she wondered aloud, 'What must she have thought?'

'The shepherds must have been a bit confused too. Imagine hearing a choir of angels then finding Jesus in a stinky stable instead of somewhere fancy,' Fran replied.

Before Ava answered, they realised they were back at the front door of the church, and the golden footprints had vanished.

'Where have you two been?' said Nan. 'It's time to put up the Christmas crib.'

Following Nan inside, they saw a model cave near the altar at the front of the church. The white-haired man who they had last seen holding holly now held up a model of a donkey and called, 'Fran, do you want to come and put the donkey in the stable? We are getting the crib ready.'

Fran laid out the prickly straw for the animals and put some in the box for the model of baby Jesus while

THE CAVE AT GRECCIO

Ava arranged the figures of Mary, Joseph and the shepherds just as they had stood in Francis's cave.

Fran gave Nan a big hug.

'You were right, Nan. This has been loads better than chocolate and watching a film.'

Nan smiled. 'Why have you changed your mind?'

'I do still like those things,' Fran admitted, 'but I'm thinking now that it is Christ's Mass and, perhaps, I need to think a bit more about the story of the first Christmas.'

Ava reached a hand to touch the figure of Mary in the Christmas crib.

'I agree with Fran. I'm going to use the crib to think about Mary. Imagine having a baby in a smelly stable! I'm not sure how much I would be smiling like this Mary.'

Ava placed the kneeling figure of Mary back in the crib.

'I imagine the sight and sounds of a new baby helped,' Nan replied, 'but I'm glad you've thought about the Christmas story some more.'

Ava and Fran both nodded.

'I think that when Saint Francis had the first Christmas crib with people and animals, he hoped to change the way people thought about Christmas even then, and he lived a long time ago, when there were no films or chocolate!' Nan said. 'I might even have a book about him and the first Christmas crib at home. I think reading it was when your mother first decided she liked the name Francis.'

Fran thought for a moment.

'Perhaps this Christmas, I can read that book instead of watching a film and learn a bit more about St Francis.'

'Me too,' Ava agreed.

> Francis (1181–1226) lived in Assisi, Italy. His family were wealthy, and Francis was expected to follow in his father's business. However, he was imprisoned for a year, leading to a period of sickness when he questioned the purpose of his life. When his father paid for Francis's freedom, Francis changed and began devoting his life to God. He gave away everything he owned and relied on gifts for food. He was followed by many others, inspired to change their lives by his example, eventually founding the religious

THE CAVE AT GRECCIO

order of the Franciscans. In 1223, he travelled to Greccio, where he acted out the nativity of Jesus. Saint Bonaventure quotes Francis saying, 'I want to do something that will recall the memory of that Child who was born in Bethlehem, to see with bodily eyes the inconveniences of his infancy, how he lay in the manger, and how the ox and ass stood by.' Francis changed Christmas celebrations by placing the picture of Jesus born into poverty and laying in a manger at the heart of the celebration.

What do you think Saint Francis means by the 'inconveniences of his infancy'? What does the story say to you about celebrating Christmas?

4
Lucky Josephine
Josephine Bakhita

'Look, Bea, you can see the dome of St Peter's ahead.' Dad pointed through the gap between the buildings. 'Did you know that it's the biggest church in the world?'

Bea shook her head, peering out under the hood of her soggy raincoat. It was her first visit to Rome. She had imagined the city in the sunshine, not the cold, dreary rain that fell today, soaking through her trainers. Her brother Sandy, who had visited with their dad before, chimed in.

'I remembered that from the last time we came. Will we see the Pope inside the church?'

Dad shook his head.

'No, the Pope will be here on Wednesday, and if it's sunny we will sit in front of St Peter's church to listen to him.'

They rounded a corner.

'Here we are.'

'It's still amazing!' Sandy gasped.

The dark dome of the church stood out against the grey-clouded sky, and the white marble columns at the front stretched up from the slate cobblestones where the rain splashed. St Peter's Square reflected the cloudy sky like a large pond. A circle of tall white columns spread out from the front of the church, wrapping the edge of the cobblestones with a covered walkway.

'Dad, why is it called St Peter's Square, when it's really a circle?' Sandy asked.

'I don't know,' Dad replied. 'Maybe it's something you could ask when we get inside.'

While they walked through a security check, Dad explained that he would get tickets to see the Pope at a Papal Audience.

A rainbow of brightly coloured umbrellas flowed from the entrance to the ticket office across the cobbles.

'Oh no! Look at the length of the queue!' groaned Dad. 'Well, if we want to see the Pope, then I suppose I should join.' He pulled a face. 'But you two can have a little explore if you like. Stay inside the colonnade, that's the name of these columns that circle the outside. Perhaps look at the statues?'

Dad pointed to the enormous white figures that stood on top of the colonnade.

'Can we go inside, Dad?' Bea grumbled. 'My feet are soaked and I'm freezing.'

'Come on, Bea, let's explore!' Sandy took hold of his sister's hand. 'We can run to warm up.'

'Alessandro,' Sandy heard the warning in Dad's voice as he used his full name, 'be careful, the cobblestones are slippery.'

Sandy rolled his eyes and stepped in slow motion with Bea to look up at the first statues.

'Who is that one, in the pointy hat?' Bea pointed at the white figure standing above them, holding a book in one hand and pointing down at her with the other. He had a curly beard, but she couldn't see his face.

Sandy shrugged. 'I think they are all saints, but I can't see their names. They are too high up.' Sandy scanned for something else to explore while Bea fiddled with her wet shoes.

'Let's go and look at that one, Bea.'

He pointed at one sculpture on the ground that looked quite different to those on top of the colonnade. It was dark and had a metallic shine in the rain. It showed lots of people piled together, as if they were climbing out of a hole in the cobbles. At the end, one figure stood alone, holding up a trapdoor as though they were freeing people who were trapped in a hole in the ground.

'It doesn't say who she is,' said Bea, 'but she looks different from the statues up there.'

Bea gestured to the white marble figures looking down at her as she investigated the determined face of the woman holding the trapdoor.

The woman's curly hair was partly hidden under a bonnet, and she wore a long dress and boots. One hand held up the trapdoor, which looked heavy, while the other reached out, as though asking for help. Bea touched the cold metal fingertips, imagining they were real.

'What's your story?' she whispered.

'Is this part of the sculpture?' Sandy pointed at a worn-out sandal on the floor. The straps were broken, and the sole was so thin it looked like it had walked for a thousand miles. Sandy picked it up, examined it, then passed it to his sister.

'Perhaps if we follow these footprints we will find out,' Bea replied as she looked at the battered sandal.

Sandy hadn't noticed the golden footprints leading away from the sculpture. He followed his sister, placing his feet into each footstep.

Bea was one step ahead of him when an elderly lady stepped in front of her.

'Oh, I'm sorry.' Bea managed to stop herself from crashing into the lady, meaning Sandy bumped into her.

'Ouch!' Bea glared at her brother. She turned to the lady.

'Sorry. We found this worn-out sandal, and we wondered if it could tell us about the lady in the sculpture, the one with the determined face.'

The lady smiled at Bea and Sandy. 'Can I see the sandal? Well, I haven't seen a sandal like this for many years.' The lady's eyes filled with tears. 'It looks like it could have belonged to Josephine Bakhita. She once had to walk almost a thousand miles, and she was only seven years old. She is the lady holding up the trapdoor in the sculpture. I met her a long time ago. Would you like to hear her story?'

Sandy and Bea nodded as the lady, who told them her name was Angelica, held the sandal, staring at it and pondering the memories it stirred.

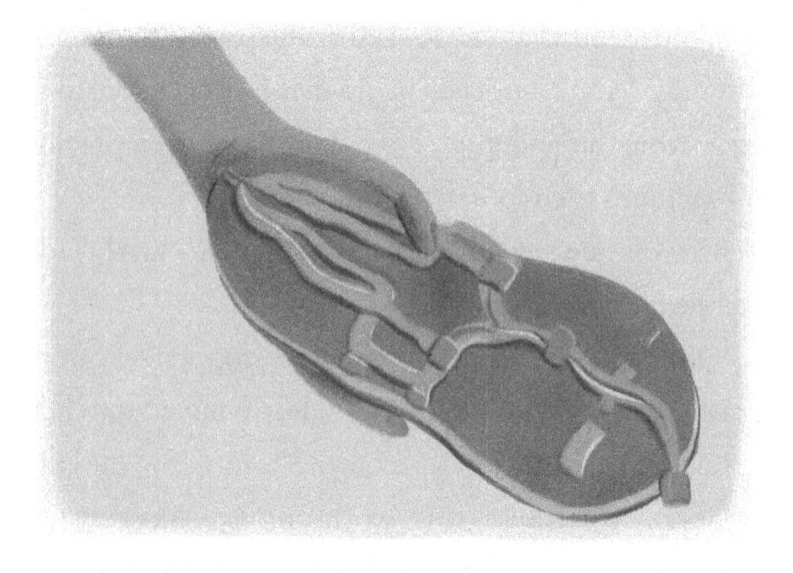

Shaking her head, the lady led them away from the hustle and bustle of people shaking out their umbrellas and chatting in the square as the rain stopped. She spread her raincoat on the sweeping stone steps that led towards St Peter's church so they could sit down.

'Well, at the start of the story, Josephine Bakhita was not her name. No one knows her original name, she forgot it.'

'How could someone forget their name?' Bea asked.

'Sometimes it hurts less to forget than to remember.' Angelica smiled sadly. 'I will call her Bakhita. She grew up in Sudan, a country in Africa. She was a happy girl whose family loved her. But, when she was around seven years old, younger than you,' Angelica nodded at Bea, 'she was kidnapped and taken away from her family by human traffickers. They made her walk so far that her sandals wore out and she walked barefoot. By the time she arrived in the city, she had forgotten her name. So, the human traffickers called her 'Bakhita', which means lucky. Do you think she felt lucky?'

Sandy shook his head. 'I thought enslavement ended after the American Civil War. I never really thought about human trafficking in the rest of the world.'

'The world is a big place,' Angelica frowned. 'Do you think you can contain the horror of one person saying "I own you" to another person to a single place in history?'

Sandy thought about this as Angelica continued the story.

'The slave traders sold Bakhita to a man who made her work as a maid for his daughters. Then, when she broke a vase, the family beat her and sold her again.'

'She was only seven!' Bea gasped, imagining a life with cruel strangers.

'She was sold again and again until, twelve years later, when she was nineteen, an Italian diplomat who lived in Sudan bought Bakhita, and she lived with his family.'

'What's a diplomat?' Sandy asked.

'In this story it means he communicated what the Italian government wanted to say to the government in Sudan. Eventually, it was time for the family to move back to Italy, and Bakhita travelled with them. When they arrived, they gave her away again to a new family who made her look after their little daughter.'

'You can't give someone away!' Sandy protested. 'People are not things. Poor Bakhita!'

'That is what human trafficking means. You are a possession, not a person,' Angelica said.

'I'm not enjoying this story, it's too sad,' Bea admitted. 'I hope she escapes from these people soon.'

Angelica smiled. 'Well, the story is going to get a bit brighter now. When the parents had to travel, they left Bakhita and their daughter with a community of nuns in Venice, in the north of Italy. Living with the nuns, Bakhita heard stories from the Gospels about how much God loved her. She felt free from her life of enslavement and begged the nuns to let her be baptised as a Christian and then eventually become a nun.'

'And did they let her?' Bea interrupted.

'Well,' Angelica continued, 'the family who believed they owned her were angry and appealed to the King of Italy to have their property returned.'

Sandy put his hands to his face. 'Oh no! I hope the King took Bakhita's side.'

'Yes, the Italian courts ruled that there were no enslaved people in Italy. Bakhita was free to stay!'

Laughing, Angelica clapped her hands and Sandy punched the air.

'The nuns agreed she could stay with them. On 9 January 1890, she was baptised Josephine Margaret Fortunata – Fortunata is the Latin translation of Bakhita.'

Bea chewed her lip. 'Angelica, is that her happy ending?'

'Well, after that the story changes. Bakhita, or Josephine we should now call her, starts changing people's hearts and minds now her enslavement has come to an end. How would you feel if people had treated you badly?' Angelica pointed at Sandy.

Sandy's eyebrows pulled down in a frown. 'Really angry. I think I'd want to get even.'

'Well, Josephine did the opposite. She always spoke of how God had shown his love to her. She was never angry with the people who had kidnapped her or those who had beaten her, saying that because of them she had been set on a path to Jesus. Her story showed people that love changes everything.'

Bea thought about how she had not thanked Dad for bringing her to Rome, moaning about her wet feet instead.

'I was a little girl in the Second World War,' said Angelica, 'and Josephine Bakhita lived in my village of Schio. She was an old lady then, almost as old as I am now. We believed that her prayers protected our village because when it was bombed, no one died. Josephine spent her life telling people her story and helping them understand that enslavement was not something in the past.'

'So, she showed how she changed her life of enslavement into a life full of love,' said Sandy. 'I suppose that's why she was setting people free in the statue we looked at, because she knew what it was like to be treated as if she didn't matter.'

Angelica nodded. 'Maybe look at her face now and think why she looks so determined?'

'Yes! Let's look again. Do you want to come with us?' asked Bea.

Angelica shook her head. 'Off you go, I will sit here a little longer. The sun is starting to shine.'

Bea and Sandy followed the footprints back to the statue.

'Alessandro! Beatrice!' They heard their dad's voice calling.

Sandy waved, and their father walked over to join them.

Bea wrapped her arms around him. 'Thank you, Dad, for bringing me to Rome, and for being my dad.'

Dad laughed. 'What's brought this on?'

'Well,' Sandy replied, 'this statue is of Josephine Bakhita. We met a lady who told us how she was stolen from her family.'

'She is setting people free because she was enslaved when she was a little girl,' Bea interrupted.

'How interesting.' Dad peered at the statue. 'I think this is going to be a story worth hearing.'

> Pope St John Paul II named Josephine Bakhita (1869-1947) a saint in 2000. Her extraordinary life showed how a victim of human trafficking could change her life by focusing on the good things she had experienced in spite of the terrible trauma she suffered. Josephine dedicated the rest of her life to serving God and humanity. Although she never learnt to read or write, she told her story to others. Josephine saw the whole of her life as God's gift. She also said that if she met the people who had kidnapped her in childhood, she would forgive them and kiss them.
>
> The sculpture Bea and Sandy see in St Peter's Square is by Canadian artist Timothy Schmalz, who uses her story to challenge and change people's understanding of human trafficking

LUCKY JOSEPHINE

today. The sculpture is now located close to Bakhita's grave in Schio, Italy.

👣 **What do you find inspiring about Josephine's story?**
Do you think it is always easy to forgive people?

5
Saint of the Broom
Martin de Porres

'Please, can you move?' asked Mum. 'I need to put some sheets on the bed.'

'OK, but where can we go?' Adie asked, hoping the answer would not be 'outside' because the day was too hot. Today was moving day, and though part of Adie wanted to explore the new city, another part wanted to curl up in bed with a book until all the unpacking was done.

'Why don't you and Rafe go for a walk with Papi Toni?' Mum suggested. 'Or you could stay here and mop the floor?'

Adie groaned. A choice between two dull things was not a choice at all.

Papi Toni soon had his two grandchildren walking down the street.

'Our first adventure in a new city! Where shall we explore?' Papi asked, looking at the children under the brim of his sunhat.

'Is there a mall here?' Rafe asked. 'That would be OK.'

'No thanks!' Adie frowned. She hated malls, too much noise, bright lights and people.

'Or what about this church?' Papi said as they turned the corner of the street. 'It's bound to be interesting.'

Rafe made a fake yawning face, but Adie felt pleased. Churches had fascinating pictures and windows of coloured glass, plus they would be out of the burning sun. Papi held open the heavy wooden doors as Adie and Rafe squeezed past him and into the church.

'Oh wow!' breathed Rafe, thoughts of the mall slipping from his head. 'It's beautiful in here.'

Adie nodded her agreement as Papi stepped into the church behind them, closing the door and blocking out the last of the bright sunlight. It took moments for her eyes to adjust to the dark interior of the church. The sunshine filtered through the blue light of the stained-glass windows, and Adie felt goosebumps on her arms, suddenly chilly but also excited.

'Papi,' she whispered, 'can we explore?'

'Yes,' said Papi, 'but be respectful, this is a place of prayer, not a playground.'

He pressed a coin each into the children's hands.

'Light a candle and say a prayer for your busy mama.'

Papi sat in one of the benches that lined the inside of the church. Pulling rosary beads from his pocket, he closed his eyes, his lips moving in silent prayer.

Adie and Rafe walked down the centre of the church, which was lined with stone arches reaching towards the roof on either side. Above them, a bright blue ceiling illuminated with golden stars arced upwards.

Rafe gazed up. 'That's amazing. It's like the shape of an upside-down boat.' He touched the tips of his fingers together, making the roof shape.

They walked towards the vast window that seemed to fill a whole wall, and then Adie saw candlelight flicker at the side of the church.

'Come on.' She pulled Rafe under one of the enormous stone archways. 'Let's light a candle like Papi said.'

They walked towards the side of the church, where a large metal tray filled with sand stood before a statue. Candles were stuck into the sand. One or two still gave a flickering light, but most had burned away, leaving a tiny stump of wax.

Adie put her coin into a tin with a slot and reached for a new candle from a wooden table next to the sand tray.

'Hang on a minute,' Rafe said. 'Are you sure this is a place to say prayers?'

'Why?' asked Adie, placing her candle in the tray.

'Because when I've been in churches before, the statues are of Mary, the mother of Jesus, or saints holding a cross or rosary. I've never seen one holding a mop!'

Adie looked up at the statue. It showed a man with smiling eyes, black hair and brown skin wearing a long, white robe. Around his shoulders was a black cape, and in his hand was a mop.

SAINT OF THE BROOM

'Maybe he is the saint of mopping!' Rafe giggled.

'And he's got work to do – look at these shiny footprints someone has left across the floor,' Adie sniggered.

At the end of the footprints was a man wearing a long, white robe, like the statue, sweeping mud and straw from the church floor.

'See,' said Rafe. 'It's a cleaner's uniform.'

'Excuse me!' he shouted. 'We are looking for information about a statue. We don't think it can be a saint because he is holding a mop. I mean, he can't be a saint of mopping!'

The man stopped sweeping the floor and stared at Rafe.

'Do you think cleaning is not important, young man?'

Sensing Rafe might have upset the man, Adie answered, 'We just thought statues are usually of Jesus or Mary or about a saint who prayed a lot. I'm Adriana, and this is my brother Raphael, Adie and Rafe for short.'

'Good morning to you both,' the man replied. 'My name is Juan. I am curious to know what you think praying looks like?'

'I think you join your hands and say a prayer like the "Our Father",' suggested Rafe.

'Or,' Adie continued, 'our Papi prays with rosary beads. He usually sits or kneels. I think praying is quiet.'

'Ah, then you don't think that sweeping the straw and mud from the floor as I am doing can be a type of prayer? Perhaps you need to learn a little bit about Martin, the man who inspired me to be a priest,' Juan replied. 'He taught me how you can make your whole life a prayer. If in everything you do, you raise a heart full of love for God, then mopping the floor or cutting someone's hair can be a prayer.'

'Sit.' Juan gestured to a bench. 'Listen to my story about Martin.'

'Martin was born in the city of Lima. His father was a wealthy man from Spain. His mama had been set free from enslavement. But his father deserted the family, so his mama had to earn money and bring up Martin and his sister alone.'

'We only have a mama,' said Rafe. 'Our father left too.'

Juan nodded. 'Then you know how much a mama does to look after her children. Though Martin's mama was no longer enslaved, she was not allowed to do lots of jobs because she was from a mixed ethnic background, her parents had been African and indigenous enslaved people. In the end, she washed people's clothes for pennies.

'The family struggled to have enough money to live. Martin got a job when he was only twelve. He was apprenticed to a barber surgeon who didn't just cut hair but also did things like pulling out rotten teeth. Doctors and dentists were very expensive! So, Martin learnt a lot about caring for sick people alongside cutting men's hair. He also learnt how to sweep and mop the hair or blood from the shop floor at the end of each day.'

Adie thought she shouldn't complain about tidying her bedroom.

'Martin had a great love for God, and after a long day at work, he would spend hours each night in prayer even though he was tired to his very bones.'

Juan smiled thoughtfully, then asked, 'Do you know what a Christian monk is?'

'Some sort of priest I think,' said Adie.

'Who wear long, brown dresses, tied with a rope,' Rafe added.

'In Christianity, they are a community of men who chose to give up their possessions, live like brothers and offer their lives in the service of God. Not all monks wear brown, they can wear different colours, and it's called a habit, not a dress. Christian monks also shave part of their head, it is called a tonsure.' Juan tipped his head, showing the children his circular bald spot.

'Shaving needs a barber and Martin began to spend a lot of time at the Holy Rosary Priory, which was the name for the religious brothers' house, in Lima. He felt God calling him to join the community, but he faced a big problem. The rules of the Priory said Martin could not join because he was from a mixed ethnic family.'

'No way!' Rafe blurted out.

'That is unfair,' Adie agreed.

'What did he say to them?' Rafe continued. 'Did he say he didn't think much of their stupid rules?'

'Is that what you would do?' Juan asked.

Rafe nodded.

'Me too!' Juan admitted. 'But Martin saw the rejection as a way to change people's attitudes and help them understand that he wanted to give his life to God.

SAINT OF THE BROOM

Aged fifteen, he gave up his barber's job and worked as a servant at the Priory. Martin did laundry, cooked and cleaned for the brothers, doing his best, with a heart full of love for God. He even continued to cut their hair!

'The brothers ran a hospital attached to the Priory. Martin cleaned there too, and used the skills he learnt as a barber-surgeon to help the sick recover. As time passed, people noticed how caring Martin was for sick people. Sometimes, those he looked after recovered when others had given up hope. People began to whisper that God performed miraculous healings through Martin's prayers. Eventually, after eight years, the Prior in charge at Holy Rosary decided to bend the rules and allow Martin to join the brothers. Martin joined the Order of Saint Dominic, becoming one of over three hundred brothers who lived at the Priory. Some of the brothers thought the Prior was wrong. They called Martin names because of the colour of his skin and because his mother had been enslaved. It was tough for him.'

'They bullied Martin because he was different.' Rafe's voice shook, and his eyes brimmed with tears.

Adie squeezed her brother's arm, remembering the names he had been called at school when he started wearing spectacles.

Juan smiled at Rafe. 'Jesus teaches that we should love our neighbours, but Martin knew it was not always easy! Martin had a pet dog, a cat and a tiny mouse. He fed them all from the same dish to show the brothers that if animals could get on when they experienced kindness, why couldn't the brothers?

'Martin spent his time working in the hospital and became well known as a healer. One day, a beggar in the street asked for his help. The man was filthy and covered with sores. Because he knew there was no room at the hospital, Martin let the man sleep in his bed. When one of the brothers complained that Martin had brought somebody grubby back to their living place, Martin said that charity is more important than cleanliness. You see, he lived his life in the most loving way possible.

'Eventually, the Prior put Martin in charge of the hospital. He made sure that everyone received the same treatment, whether rich or poor, an enslaved person or a duke. He continued doing his old work, like cleaning the floor, because a clean hospital is essential. He

SAINT OF THE BROOM

stopped eating meat and gave this part of his food to people who were hungry.'

'Did the other brothers ever stop bullying him?' Adie asked.

'I'm sure he still met mean people,' Juan replied, 'but when Martin died, his goodness was known throughout the city and many people came to pray at his funeral.'

'He changed people's minds by behaving in an opposite way to them, being kind where they were cruel and doing simple jobs like cleaning instead of trying to make himself important,' said Rafe.

Juan nodded. 'Speaking of which, I'd better get back to

my cleaning. I've only swept the straw and mud from the floor, it still needs mopping. What would Martin say?'

Laughing, Rafe and Adie said thank you to Juan then followed the footprints back towards the statue of Martin. Adie lit the candle she had placed in the sand and prayed a thank you prayer for her mama.

'Hey!' Papi called. 'Did you get lost?'

'No, we have been learning about this man, Martin,' explained Rafe. 'We followed these footprints . . .'

But the footprints had disappeared.

'Saint Martin de Porres,' Papi read the label under the statue. 'Why is he holding a mop?'

'We will tell you on the way home,' laughed Adie. 'But I think it's time we helped mama.'

Martin de Porres (1579–1639) grew up in poverty and was not considered good enough to join the Dominican religious order. He lived in Lima in Peru. Before he was allowed to become a Dominican, one of his nicknames was the 'saint of the broom'. He changed perceptions about a person with a mixed ethnic background being allowed to join the monastery and showed that someone who led a humble life could be close to God.

> How did Martin challenge people's ideas about race and poverty in his own time? Thinking about Martin's life, how would you answer the question, 'What makes someone a saint?'

6
Blessed are the Poor?
The Beatitudes based on Matthew chapter 5

'B-L-E-S-S-E-D' Jo spelt the massive word across the centre of the new display in the school corridor.

'But what does blessed mean?' Jude asked. 'And what about all these other words, righteousness and merciful? I'm not sure what this new display is about at all.'

Jo and Jude looked at the words on the wall before them. The words formed the shape of a giant cloud, criss-crossing each other, and the word BLESSED was in blue capital letters across the centre.

'It says "kingdom of heaven" there,' Jo pointed. 'Perhaps it's something to do with God?'

'Maybe,' Jude replied. 'Look, there is a label here that says, "Find out more about the Beatitudes" and a tiny golden footprint.'

'There are more footprints on the floor. Let's see where they go,' Jude suggested.

Jo and Jude followed the footprints, which were glowing slightly.

'Do you think they used luminous paint for these?' Jude reached down to touch the footprints.

Jo shrugged as she opened a door.

'I haven't been through this door before either. Have you? I thought it was a cupboard.'

Jo stopped speaking as, surprisingly, she found herself outside.

'Where are we?' Jude asked, following Jo through the door. 'This isn't the school playing field.'

'And who are all those people?' Jo answered Jude's question with a question. 'Their clothes are like something out of the Bible.'

The footprints had brought them towards a crowd who seemed to be walking away from something, like people leaving a football match, all heading in the same direction. People were talking and waving their arms as if what they had heard had given them lots to discuss.

Jude and Jo approached two men who stood in deep conversation.

'Shall we ask them about the footprints? Has our teacher arranged a theatre group or something? Did we find them earlier than we were supposed to?' Jo whispered. 'Why else would they be wearing those robes?'

One wore a blue and white striped robe, like a long, flowing dress, with full-length sleeves and a wide red fabric belt tied around his middle. He pointed his finger at the other man as though they were arguing. The other man's robe was darker, and he wore what looked like a striped scarf across his shoulders. He walked with a long stick in his left hand.

'You Pharisees are just not open to new ideas, Jacob!' the man in the striped robe said, jabbing his finger towards the other man.

'That is not true, Benjamin!' the man called Jacob almost shouted. 'I just don't understand what Jesus meant. What does "blessed are the poor" even mean?'

'Excuse me,' Jude asked, but the man called Benjamin waved Jude away.

Jude raised his voice. 'We wondered if you could help us?'

The men stopped talking abruptly and stared at Jude. Jacob folded his arms and raised an eyebrow.

'We also want to know what blessed means, please,' Jo chimed in. 'We followed some golden footprints, and they led us to you. Can you help?'

Jo suddenly felt uncertain as the men glared at her, and she realised she wasn't sure how to find the door back to school.

The man called Jacob's face relaxed into a broad smile. 'Well, we were just talking about the same thing. Let's sit here and talk about it together?'

Jacob lowered himself cross-legged onto the grass, resting his staff across his knees. Benjamin gave a short barking laugh and did the same. Jude shrugged his shoulders and sat down.

'Jude, we might be missing the lunchtime bell. Should we go back?' Jo suggested.

'I think the footprints brought us here to learn something, and I'm all ears!' Jude replied.

Jo nodded and sat on the yellowed, prickly grass, dried out by the sun. She noticed that they sat at the bottom of a hill and there seemed to be a large lake in the distance.

'Are you followers of Jesus?' Benjamin asked. 'Did you come here to meet him?'

'Not really,' Jo admitted. 'I know a bit about Jesus from my Nan's stories.'

'He is a carpenter's son from Nazareth who has started teaching and healing people miraculously, so I'm told,' Jacob grumbled. 'Benjamin thinks he is someone special, so I came to listen to him talk. But what he said didn't make sense to me.'

'Jacob, will you let me tell the story? Then we can debate his teaching!' Benjamin sounded a little cross, but his eyes smiled with excitement.

'Jesus is from Nazareth and worked as a carpenter, like his father. What Jacob says is true. But I believe

God has called him in some unique way I don't yet fully understand. He has a group of followers, some who were fishermen on Lake Galilee. They listened to him, then suddenly left everything they had to follow Jesus. Can you imagine that? He has been travelling around the shore of Lake Galilee, which is a lot of walking.' Benjamin pointed to the distant lake.

'He teaches as he travels, helping people understand the stories of Moses and the prophets and sometimes healing people who are in pain or have a disease. Now, Jesus is famous. People have heard of him in Jerusalem, Judea, and even as far away as Syria.'

'Benjamin and I have travelled from Jerusalem. Have you come far?' Jacob asked.

'We haven't walked far,' Jude replied, though he wondered how far the footprints had really helped them travel.

Jacob continued. 'We have just been listening to Jesus. He gave a talk which has left me confused. He kept saying people were blessed when they obviously were not. What does he mean by "blessed are the poor"! Do you have any idea?'

'No,' Jo admitted. 'I'm not really sure what the word blessed means.'

'Jesus' teaching is so confusing even children don't understand.' Jacob folded his arms, glaring at Benjamin.

'Perhaps that's because they have listened to you explain, Jacob,' Benjamin said with a gentle smile. 'Today, Jesus taught us about what makes us really happy. That's what he means when he says "blessed". He is talking about being happy, deeply happy, on the inside.'

'I'm not sure I understand what you mean,

Benjamin, sorry,' Jude said, his forehead creasing in concentration.

'Let's think of it this way. Have you ever really wanted something because you thought it would make your life perfect, then, when you got it, you found it was just a thing?' Benjamin asked.

Jo answered, 'Yes. I begged my mum for some new shoes because I wanted to be like everyone else, but when I got them, they were uncomfortable. I felt really disappointed and bad that Mum had saved up to treat me with some shoes I didn't wear.'

'So, they didn't make you happy, even though you thought they would?' Benjamin looked into Jo's eyes as she nodded her head.

'Jesus says we should stop wanting things and concentrate on what God wants for us. If we do this, we will be happy because loving God gives our life purpose. It makes us change and feel happy on the inside. So, Jacob, when Jesus says "blessed are the poor in spirit", I think he means that we can only become happy when we stop focusing on things we want and change by focusing on God.'

Jacob let out a big sigh. 'We are not going to agree

about this, Ben. I think that God asks us to give to people who are poor and might be suffering. We should see them as sisters and brothers who need our help. But I'm not sure that giving away all my money would make me closer to God. I don't want to be poor. When I give to poor people, I want others to see me do it and say, "Well done!" If I'm rich, it shows God has blessed me!' Jacob grabbed hold of his staff and pulled himself to his feet.

'In fact, I'm not sure why I'm even talking about this with you, Ben, or with children. I'm heading back to Jerusalem. I've heard enough about Jesus wanting to change the way we live. I'm done!'

'I think Jesus is asking us to change.' Benjamin shook his head, smiling sadly at his friend.

With that, Jacob let out a sigh of frustration and strode away from Jude, Jo and Benjamin, who were still sitting on the ground. Benjamin looked slightly stunned.

'I'm sorry he can be so grumpy. It's not easy to start to question if what you do in life brings you deep happiness, a happiness that can't be taken away.'

Benjamin paused, lost in thought.

'I will search for Jesus to see if I can find out more about this blessed life he talks about. Are you going to join me?'

'Not today,' Jo replied. 'It's time we returned, but thank you for sharing your ideas, Benjamin.'

Jo pointed at the ground. Had the footprints always been there, and they hadn't noticed? Jude stood to follow them, turning to face Benjamin.

'Good luck finding Jesus,' he smiled.

Benjamin waved goodbye and walked away as Jude and Jo followed the footprints into the school corridor.

'Jo, what just happened?' Jude asked.

'I'm not sure to be honest,' Jo answered. 'Why don't we see what we can find out about Jesus' teaching about being happy in the library?'

Mrs Cruz, the librarian, sat behind her desk, munching on a sandwich.

'Hello you two. You are looking puzzled.'

'There is something we don't understand,' Jo started.

'It's about what makes us happy,' Jude explained. 'We've just been talking to someone who said Jesus teaches that people who are poor in spirit are happy – blessed, they said.'

'Well, libraries are full of answers,' Mrs Cruz smiled. 'Let's start with the Bible, that's where you can find what Jesus said.'

Mrs Cruz brushed sandwich crumbs off her fingers and reached for a large, heavy, blue book from the shelf behind her.

'Here you are. Matthew's Gospel, chapter five: "Blessed are the poor in spirit, for theirs is the kingdom of heaven." If you look here, Jesus gives eight sayings that begin "blessed are" that are called the Beatitudes. The headteacher said she is putting a display up about them in the corridor.'

'We saw it, and it led us to someone who said that blessed means happy,' Jo explained.

Mrs Cruz nodded. 'They are a bit tricky at first because Jesus seems to be saying the opposite of what makes us happy.

'If you look at this one, "Blessed are they who mourn, for they will be comforted," it seems the wrong way around. When someone dies, we are sad because we miss them; that is called mourning. Jesus teaches that if we put our trust in God, then we know when people die, they go to be with God, so though we miss them in our lives, we shouldn't be sad. In the same way, people who seem poor in spirit are truly happy because they know what matters in life is not money but loving God. Am I making sense?'

'Oh yes!' said Jude. 'I wish I could tell Benjamin that I understand now.'

'Well,' Jo suggested, 'perhaps we could go back and look at the display and see if it now makes sense.'

'Excellent plan!' Mrs Cruz said. 'And if you still don't understand, you can always return to the library!'

'Thank you!' Jo and Jude shouted as they headed back towards the corridor.

> You can step into this story in Matthew's Gospel (Matthew 5:1–11).
>
> The Beatitudes – a set of eight statements – are part of Jesus' teachings about what makes a life blessed, or happy. In each one, Jesus gives a blessing, says something about the people he is blessing, then explains why they are blessed.
>
> So, people who embrace a life that is not

focused on money or possessions will be much closer to building a kinder world. Jesus changes the expectations in his own time and today by teaching that true happiness, or blessings, comes from placing God before personal needs and wants.

👣 **What do you think makes for a happy life?**

7

The Centurion's Servant
Luke 7:1–10

'On this site, archaeologists found the remains of a Roman house, and we are going to look at some of the things that helped them relate the finds to the Roman period.' The museum guide shouted, struggling to make herself heard over the excited chatter.

Mr Portillo raised his hand in the air, a signal for silence.

'Please settle down, class six, everyone will get a chance to look.'

Lou and Jay raised their hands, but Lou carried on talking.

'I want to see a Roman sword,' Lou whispered.

'Lou, Jay, were you two talking?' Mr Portillo tutted. 'You can look at the artefacts last, thank you.'

Jay pulled a face at Lou. Because they were partners, they would both have to wait until the end.

'OK,' Mr Portillo gestured to Jay. 'You two next.'

The museum guide smiled at Lou. 'I always got into trouble for talking too, but because you are last, you can look at things a little longer.'

The guide showed them bits of a cooking pot, a roof tile, some tiny cubes that once were part of a floor mosaic and many other things, but an oil lamp captured Jay's imagination. It was a small oval, shaped from orange clay, with a tiny handle and spout. The guide explained that a servant would fill this lamp with olive oil, and then push a thin piece of cotton or linen through the spout so it touched the oil. When the cotton was lit, the lamp would burn.

'What's really unusual about this lamp is that it has a Christian symbol. Can you see?'

She pointed to what looked like a pointy p with a letter x running through it.

'It's called the Chi-Rho symbol. That's because *chi* and *rho* are the first two letters of Christ in Greek. It suggests that the Romans who lived here were Christians.'

'I never think about the Romans being Christians. Do you?' Lou asked Jay.

'No,' Jay replied. 'I think of them following Jupiter and stuff. I suppose there are some Romans in the stories about Jesus though.'

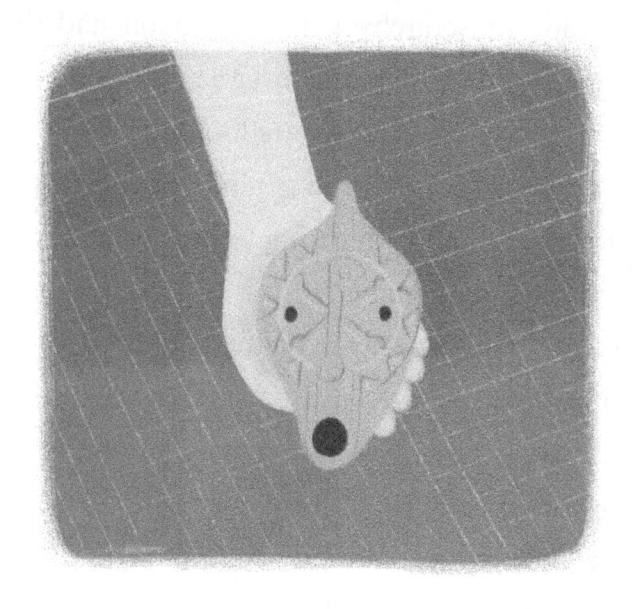

Gently lifting the tiny lamp from the artefact tray, Jay said, 'Can you imagine whose hands would have held this almost two thousand years ago?'

Before Lou could answer, they both realised the room was now empty.

'Oh no!' Jay gasped. 'Now we'll really be in trouble.'

'It's fine, we must just follow those golden footprints, they look a bit glow-in-the-dark so they must show the way,' Lou replied.

'Fine!' Jay muttered, following Lou, forgetting to replace the precious lamp.

The footprints led through a doorway covered by a curtain made of scratchy wool. A person had their back to them and was bending over a table.

'Excuse me,' Jay began, 'we are looking for—'

'Who are you? How did you get in here?' A girl spun to face them, her hand stretching to hide whatever she had been doing on the table.

Jay realised she was only a few years older than her. She also realised the girl was dressed like the Romans they had been studying, wearing a long, white tunic tied by a leather belt around her waist.

'I'm sorry if my friend made you jump,' Lou said. 'I think she meant to ask where we should go. We've been looking at the Roman stuff. In fact, my friend there, Jay, seems to still be holding on to something.'

Suddenly, remembering the lamp in her hand, Jay's words stuck in her throat as she apologised and offered the lamp to the girl.

Seeing the lamp, the girl immediately relaxed.

'Oh! You have brought a token to show you are here for the celebration.'

Stepping aside, Lou and Jay saw two identical lamps on the table, a jug and some thin strips of fabric.

'I was filling the lamps with oil ready for tonight's prayer service,' she explained. 'See, these also have the secret symbol, so I know you are followers of Christ, like me.'

She turned the lamps around, showing Lou and Jay the Chi-Rho symbol.

'I will fill yours too, then you are ready. My name is Antonia.'

'I never think of the Romans as believing in Jesus,' Lou repeated. 'I always think of the punishments, you know, like feeding people to the lions at the Colosseum in Rome.'

Antonia's face filled with horror.

'Hush.' She shook her head. 'You must not speak of it so lightly. That is why we must keep our meetings secret, especially as some people know my grandfather's history.'

Wondering who Antonia was, because she didn't seem like a museum guide, Jay asked, 'Who is your grandfather?'

'My grandfather met Jesus when he was a centurion in the village of Capernaum, near Lake Galilee, far from here.'

Lou nodded. 'I've heard of Lake Galilee, it's where Jesus called the fishermen to be his apostles, isn't it?'

'That's right!' Antonia continued. 'Well, my grandfather was a centurion in the army and heard Jesus teach. Grandfather said he had never heard anyone speak like Jesus. Instead of constantly fighting for yourself, Jesus talked about caring for others. It was a new idea for a soldier like him. He listened when Jesus said we should think of God as a loving father and call him Father in prayer. This was so different from the stories of the Roman gods my grandfather grew up with. Roman gods were like people, full of anger and jealousy and fighting for power.

Jay scratched her forehead. 'I've never really thought about that.'

'For my grandfather, it was a new idea. Then he started to hear stories that Jesus could sometimes heal people who were unwell. Grandfather wanted to listen to Jesus speak in Capernaum, but then one of his servants had a terrible fall and injured his back. He was in dreadful pain and could not move his legs properly. Everyone in the house thought he would die, but my grandfather decided to run and find Jesus. Amazingly, Jesus was just walking into Capernaum when my grandfather bumped into him. Grandfather begged Jesus to help. Jesus said he would come to the house, but Grandfather stopped him.'

'Why would he do that?' Jay asked.

'Well, Grandfather said he oversaw other soldiers, and when he gave commands, they did as he told them to do. So, he said to Jesus, "Lord, I am not worthy that you should come under the roof of my house. Just say the word, and my servant will be healed."

'Jesus was really surprised at how much Grandfather believed in him, more than anyone else he had met. Jesus sent Grandfather home, saying because of his great faith, he would find the servant healed when he got there. When Grandfather returned, no one in the house could explain how a man could be screaming in pain one minute, then walking around absolutely fine the next.'

To hear more, Lou asked, 'Antonia, what did they think when your grandfather told them about Jesus?'

'At first, no one believed him. Why would a Jewish teacher help a Roman soldier? As time passed, however, and people heard more stories about Jesus, they began to think Grandfather was right, there had been a miracle.'

'Did they all follow Jesus, like you?' Jay asked.

'Not everyone who hears stories about Jesus decides to follow his teaching. My family became followers of Christ when my grandfather started sharing his story and met other people who believed Jesus was more than an ordinary man.

'When our family was posted here, at the edge of the Roman Empire, we continued to follow Christ and met other believers. But I don't have time to tell you all about that today. I must get the room ready for the prayers tonight. We will gather here this evening to pray, tell stories about Jesus and share a simple meal. You are welcome to join us.' Antonia smiled at them.

'Thanks,' said Lou. 'Do we just follow the footprints?'

Antonia had turned back to the lamps, but Jay nodded, and they left the room, following the footprints back the way they had come.

'Do you think that was part of the museum?' Jay wondered.

'I hope so because we left the lamp!' Lou frowned, realising Antonia had filled it with oil.

'Catch up, you two!' Mr Portillo barked from the end of the corridor.

They followed Mr Portillo down some steps into what seemed to be a dimly lit cellar.

'I'm going to put a bright light on for a few minutes,' the museum guide said.

Blinking against the sudden dazzle, Lou saw crumbling old walls in front of him, and the room suddenly made sense.

'Do you think these are the remains of a Roman house?' Jay said a bit too loudly.

'That's right, well done,' the guide said. 'In fact, it was here that the lamp you looked at earlier was found with the Chi-Rho symbol. Many Romans had household altars, but the one we found here had the Chi-Rho painted on the east-facing wall, which suggests that the family were Christians.'

'No way!' Lou exclaimed. 'Would they have hidden the fact that they followed Jesus?'

The guide smiled at their interest. 'Probably, but we don't know for sure. We can work out that the family were Christians because of the things they left behind, but we don't know their story.'

'I think we could tell you a good story, couldn't we, Lou?' Jay smiled.

You can step into this story in Luke's Gospel (Luke 7:1–10, also Matthew 8:5–13).

Capernaum was a fishing and farming community on the northwest shore of Lake Galilee. In Jesus' time, it was controlled by King Herod Antipas, a Jewish king ruled by the Roman Empire. The centurion in the story is likely to have been working with Herod rather than in charge of a group of Roman soldiers, so he lived in the village.

THE CENTURION'S SERVANT

Luke started to write down his Gospel about fifty years after Jesus' death and resurrection. By this time, there were Christian communities in Rome, parts of Greece and North Africa, which were all part of the Roman Empire. Christianity spread through families and small communities gathering at home to pray, share stories of Jesus and break bread. These followers changed their religious beliefs and gradually Christianity spread, changing the Roman Empire. Luke uses this story to show that Jesus' message is for everyone.

Jesus says that he has never found faith like the centurion's. What do you think it means to 'have faith'? How do you think the story encourages people to have faith?

8
The Hole in the Roof
Luke 5:17–26

'If you want to come back to my house, we can do our homework together?' Taz suggested.

Zak thought for a moment before replying. Taz's dad was still building their house. It could be pretty noisy with hammering or drilling, and sometimes the electricity didn't work.

'Will we have Wi-Fi at your house today? Should we go to the library instead?'

'Oh yes! Dad promises everything is nearly finished.' Taz smiled. 'It will be fun working on this project together.'

'I'm not sure I'm ever going to find researching houses at the time of Jesus actually interesting,' said Zak, 'but your mum does usually have chocolate biscuits and we won't be able to eat those at the library.'

Zak unwrapped his biscuit while Taz's mum logged into her computer so they could start their research.

'No touching the keyboard with chocolate hands, you two, OK?'

Taz made a 'mumm 'kay' noise, her mouth full of biscuit.

'I'm going to the shops before I go to work. Your dad is doing stuff to the house outside, so you will have to go and find him if you need anything. The parental controls are turned on, so just for homework.' She pointed at the computer.

'Thanks for the biscuit and for helping us,' Zak answered as Taz nodded her head.

'Where do we start?' Zak asked as Taz's mum left the room.

Taz shrugged and started to pull her homework folder out of her school bag. Opening it on the table, they looked at the project outline. It read, *'Understanding the Gospels. We are discovering how life was lived at the time of Jesus. We will learn about how people cooked, ate and lived. Your part in this project is to find out about the houses most people lived in and then make a model to show in school.'*

'Why didn't we get cooking?' Taz groaned.

As Taz put her fingers on the computer's keyboard, the screen went blank.

'Great! Looks like we are going to the library after all.' Zak reached for his school bag.

'Let's see if we can find my dad outside first,' Taz suggested. 'He might just need to flick a switch or something.'

Taz led the way outside into what would eventually be the garden.

'Which way shall we go?' Zak looked around the slabs of paving stones stacked up and the large sacks that rested against them, silently wishing that they had just gone to the library.

'Dad, there's no electricity again!' Taz bellowed.

No answer came.

'Maybe if we follow these golden footprints?' Zak suggested. 'Perhaps your dad stood in some paint and they will take us to him?'

'I'm not sure why Dad would be using gold-coloured paint, but it's a good idea,' Taz replied as she continued to shout for her dad.

They walked around the side of the house and saw white steps that seemed to lead to the roof. The footprints led up the steps.

'I don't remember any stairs here before,' Taz muttered. 'It's no wonder this house is never finished, he keeps adding extra bits. Dad, where are you?'

Taz started up the steps. Zak was not so sure he enjoyed high places.

'Shall I wait here?' he called after Taz, but she was already halfway up the steps.

Reluctantly, Zak followed, thinking about the comfy chairs in the library. Reaching the flat roof space, he felt sure this was no longer Taz's house. There was something that looked like a camp bed at one side and beside it a cloth spread out covered in fruit, perhaps to eat or dry in what was now a scorching sun.

Zak thought about pulling off his school sweater but saw Taz talking to a man and waving him to join her. Unsure about being so high up, Zak took a deep breath and stepped across the flat white roof to where Taz stood. To Zak's horror, they were both standing by a big hole in the roof.

'Oh my!' Zak sat down.

'Are you OK, Zak? You've gone a funny colour,' Taz said. 'This man doesn't know where Dad is. He thought we were looking for Jesus.' She stifled a laugh.

THE HOLE IN THE ROOF

'Jesus?' Zak repeated, pulling off his school sweater. 'Why are you talking about him?'

'Everyone is talking about Jesus!' said the man. 'That's why I've got this big hole in the roof.'

'I'm not sure if it is being high up, but I'm flummoxed,' Zak said. 'Please, will you explain what you mean?'

'You must have heard of Jesus from Nazareth,' the man said. 'He has been travelling around, teaching, telling stories, performing miracles.'

'We've heard of Jesus, but we don't understand what he has got to do with this hole in the roof!' Taz explained.

'Well, pass me that straw and help me mix it into that bucket of mud and I will tell you.'

Taz tucked the bundle of straw the man pointed towards under one arm and helped Zak carry the heavy bucket of mud with the other. They sat beside the hole, breaking the straw into smaller pieces while the man mixed it into the mud with a stick and began his story.

'Jesus was coming to this village, and everyone was excited; it was all people were talking about. People were travelling here from all around Galilee, Judea and Jerusalem, including some Pharisees and other clever people who know lots about our religious laws. My wife said, "Ethan, why not invite Jesus here for something to eat? We have plenty of room for him and his followers." So, I waited by the lakeshore, and when one of the boats with his followers arrived, I invited them to come and eat at my house. But I didn't realise how famous Jesus was. He came into our house and sat down with his friends, then the Pharisees, the teachers of the Law and other people I hadn't invited

THE HOLE IN THE ROOF

followed him. The house was so packed you could hardly move.

'People squeezed inside the room, crammed the courtyard and filled the road to the house. Everyone wanted Jesus' attention. When he spoke, everyone fell silent. We wanted to listen to what he had to say. Before he got going, there was a kerfuffle outside as people were trying to get in, but no one was letting them get closer to Jesus. Things started to settle down again when there was a noise from the roof like a hundred rats scratching. Then, bits of straw and mud began to fall on the people sitting before Jesus. I squashed and squeezed my way out, ran up the stairs and came onto this roof.'

'Oh no! Did you see a thousand rats?' Zak asked.

'No, there were no rats. Pass me those canes and I'll tell you.'

Zak passed Ethan a bundle of long canes, which he started to carefully lay on top of the thick beams of wood that criss-crossed the hole.

'I saw,' Ethan continued, 'four men pulling away the earthy plaster and canes that sat across the wooden beams of my roof to make a big hole. There was another man lying down on a stretcher. I shouted,

"Hey what are you lot doing?" One of them answered, "We've brought our friend to see Jesus. We want Jesus to heal him, to change his life." As I walked over, they started lowering their friend through the hole using ropes. They shouted, "Help him, Jesus! Heal him!" Looking at the mess they had made, I thought they must be desperate to see Jesus, so I grabbed a rope and helped them.'

'What did Jesus do?' Zak asked, feeling sick at the idea of being lowered through the hole in front of him on a wobbly rope.

'And I don't understand why the man was on a stretcher. Was he sick?' said Taz.

'The man couldn't walk, he was paralysed,' Ethan explained as he began to press mud and straw from the bucket on top of the canes, sealing the hole. 'He might have injured his back or his neck or he might have been born that way, I don't know. But I was surprised when Jesus said, "Your sins are forgiven" to the man now lying on the floor.'

Taz interrupted Ethan again. 'Did Jesus make him better? Why would he say his sins are forgiven?'

'What happens next sort of explains that,' Ethan said.

THE HOLE IN THE ROOF

Taz smiled and put a finger on her lips.

'The next thing you know, some of the Pharisees started muttering, "Who does Jesus think he is? Only God can forgive sins." One of the teachers of the Law started complaining, "This man's illness must be because he has sinned. What is Jesus saying?" Jesus knew what they were thinking, and he stopped them.'

Ethan started to press the mud and straw flat with his hands and Taz began to help him.

'Jesus said, "What are these thoughts you have in your hearts? Which is easier to say, 'Your sins are forgiven you' or to say, 'Get up and walk?'"'

'It's easier to say that you've forgiven a sin because no one can see that, but if you tell someone to get up and walk, then they've got to be able to do it.' Zak realised he was speaking aloud and mouthed 'Sorry' to Ethan.

'You are right,' continued Ethan. 'So when Jesus told the man to get up, pick up his stretcher and go home, what do you think happened?'

Taz replied, happy to speak again, 'I think he got up and walked home, because Jesus had healed him.'

'That is what happened,' Ethan smiled. 'My house has never seen so much laughter and amazement. Unfortunately, he didn't miraculously mend my roof though!'

Ethan patted the last bit of the mud and straw into place.

'Another bucket and it will be as good as new. I'm going to head off and collect some before sunset. Are you two heading home?'

Taz felt as though she was waking up from a dream. They had been looking for her dad but ended up talking to Ethan.

THE HOLE IN THE ROOF

'Taz, I think we maybe need to follow the footprints home.' Zak climbed shakily to his feet. 'I think I'd like to be on the ground again anyway.'

As they walked around the corner of the house, seeing the lawnmower reassured them they were back in Taz's garden.

Taz's dad appeared.

'I've turned the electricity back on, but I don't know Mum's password to turn on her computer. Sorry.'

'It's OK, Dad. We could go to the library instead?' Taz looked at Zak.

'Or we could have another biscuit?' Zak smiled. 'And talk about how Jesus changed the sick man's life. Why didn't he heal him straight away?'

'It's what upset the Pharisees, the sin part. It's easy to say you've forgiven someone, but no one can see inside your heart and mind if it is true.'

'I suppose so,' Zak replied. 'Perhaps ideas about illness were different in Jesus' time. Let's look it up at the library tomorrow.'

Taz agreed.

'In the meantime, I think I could draw a picture of how to fix a roof at the time of Jesus. That should keep our teacher happy that we've started our homework.'

You can step into this story in Luke's Gospel (Luke 5:17–26).

People's understanding about illnesses were very different at the time of Jesus. Often, it was believed a serious illness was because a person had done something wrong, and they were being punished. Today, science can tell us the causes of many illnesses. Jesus challenges and changes the teachings around illness and disability through his miraculous healing and by forgiving the man. In forgiving the man, Jesus shows that God is not angry with him; in healing the man, Jesus reveals his own divine power.

The house in the story is typical of most people's homes in Jesus' time. Houses were box-shaped and made of wood, stone and mud. They had few windows to help keep the house cool, so the flat roof was essential because people used it for jobs that needed good light, such as preparing food. On hot

THE HOLE IN THE ROOF

nights, families might sleep outside. Most houses had an outside staircase or ladder to get to the roof. Inside the house, there were raised platforms for sitting or sleeping but minimal furniture. People sat on cushions and mats.

The man's friends go to a lot of trouble to help him meet Jesus. What would you do to help a friend in need?

9

The Forgiving Father
Luke 15:11–32

'It's so unfair!' Ruth snarled. 'You always get to choose, just because you're the eldest.'

'That's not true!' Adam shouted. 'Dad said it was my turn to choose the treat.'

Ruth sat at the bottom of the staircase with her arms folded. She had asked to spend the afternoon drawing but now they had to go out.

'We've even had to walk down these stupid stairs because the stupid lift is broken.'

'Ruth, I hope that isn't you calling things stupid, and who was shouting?' Dad walked down the staircase behind her. 'Now, let's go to the carnival. It's Adam's turn to choose the treat.'

Adam smiled triumphantly. 'I'm going to have fun!'

Ruth rolled her eyes and checked her drawing pencils were in her rucksack, just in case.

The autumn sun shone as they walked towards the enormous public gardens and the carnival. Ruth felt her bad mood lift a little. She hoped they could go on some of the fairground rides.

'I think we should go to the "Learn about nature" exhibition along the river,' Adam suggested. 'What do you think, Dad?'

'Perhaps you should take turns to choose?' Dad suggested. 'As long as you let me know where you are going, we can arrange a time to meet up.'

'Look, there's a sign to the art tent. I'm going there!' Ruth grinned at her brother and set off running.

Unfortunately, she ran so fast that she tripped over what seemed to be a golden footprint sticking out of the grass as a sign.

'Ruth, are you OK?' Adam's hand reached down to help his sister up. 'Maybe sandals are not the best running shoes.'

'I'm fine,' Ruth lied as her knees throbbed in pain. 'I just slipped when I bent down to look at this sign.'

'Look, there are more footprints on the grass. I think we should see where they lead. It might be somewhere exciting?' Adam suggested.

'Or it might just be to those stupid trees.' Ruth pointed at the giant trees at the edge of the exhibition space.

'Maybe the trees won't seem stupid if we go and explore,' Adam offered. 'Maybe you could draw them?'

The footprints led under the shade of the trees. A man was sitting, eyes closed, next to a small table. On the table, there seemed to be some old-fashioned writing materials: dip pens made from reeds, some rough, homemade paper, and a dish of black powder.

'This grass is sticking in my sandals,' Ruth muttered.

'Quietly, Ruth, you might wake the man up,' Adam said. 'I think it looks interesting, maybe we will learn about writing a long time ago.'

The man opened his eyes and looked at them both.

'I wish I could write. I'm stuck now, trying to find the best words. I don't want to waste any papyrus making mistakes.'

'Wow! Actual papyrus! Please can I look?' Adam felt the slightly rough surface of the paper and could see the layers of plant fibre beneath the surface.

'Why are you here?' Ruth asked. 'What are you writing and how are you stuck?'

'Goodness, you are quite direct!' the man replied. 'Let me introduce myself. My name is Luke, and I am writing down some stories.'

'Oh, I like stories! Tell me and I will help you,' Ruth promised, reaching into her rucksack for her sketch book and pencils.

'Ruth, we should leave Luke to do his work and stop bothering him.'

'Adam, I'm not bothering him, I'm helping, you can go away if you like.'

Adam glared at his sister. 'Would you like to tell us your story, Luke?'

Luke nodded. 'It's a story Jesus told but no one wrote it down. I think we need to write it down because people change stories as they retell them, or sometimes stories are forgotten. It would be terrible if that happened, Jesus was a wonderful storyteller.'

Ruth and Adam sat under the shade of the tree, listening as Luke began.

'A man had two sons. The younger son said to his father, "Father, let me have the share of your property that would come to me." So, the father divided everything he had between his two sons.'

'Why did the younger son do that?' Ruth wondered.

THE FORGIVING FATHER

'Well,' Luke continued, 'perhaps the younger son didn't get on so well with his family. You know, sometimes families don't agree about things. Because the next thing the younger son did was to leave home for a distant country and spend all the money enjoying himself.'

'That doesn't sound too bad if he was having a good time,' Ruth said.

'Except,' Adam replied, 'it's not a good idea to spend all your money on fun, he should have thought about buying food, or being sure he had somewhere to live.'

'On boring things!' Ruth whispered.

'If you let me continue with the story, perhaps you can decide which idea is best,' Luke smiled.

'Having spent all his money then, the country where the younger son was living experienced a serious famine and he started to feel the pinch. He went to work for one of the local people who put him on his farm to feed the pigs.'

'Does "feel the pinch" mean he is hungry?' Ruth asked. 'He looks tired and hungry in my picture.'

Luke smiled at the drawing. 'He was so hungry, he would have happily eaten the husks they fed to the pigs, but no one offered him anything. He came to his senses, thinking, "How many of my Father's servants have more than they want to eat, and I am here, dying of hunger!" So, he made a plan.'

Ruth butted in again. 'He went home? That's boring.'

Adam answered, 'Think about it, Ruth, how will his family react? Do you think they will be pleased to see him?'

'Well,' Luke spoke before Ruth could reply, 'he prepared a speech. He intended to say, "Father, I have sinned against heaven and against you; I no longer deserve to be called your son; treat me as one of your paid servants." He headed back home. While he was

THE FORGIVING FATHER

still a long way from his home, his father saw him and was moved with pity. He ran towards the boy, hugged him and kissed him.'

'His father must have been watching for him if he saw him from a long way off,' Adam suggested.

Luke nodded. 'His son then started his speech, "Father, I have sinned against heaven and against you; I no longer deserve to be called your son—" But his father interrupted him, calling out to his servants to bring the best robe for his son, to put a ring on his finger and sandals on his feet. He told them to plan a great celebration because his son was lost and now, he was found.'

'And they all lived happily ever after!' Ruth cheered, showing them both her picture of the father and son hugging.

'Not quite, I think you may have forgotten another character in the story. Do you know who I mean?' Luke looked towards Adam.

Adam nodded. 'He had a big brother who might not have been as happy to see him as their dad.'

'Exactly!' Luke replied. 'The elder son was working out in the fields when his brother returned. As he got close to the house, he heard music and saw people dancing. He asked one of the servants what was going on. The servant explained, "Your brother has come home, and your father has ordered a grand celebration because he was lost, and now he is found." The elder brother was angry and refused to come in. His father came out to plead with him.'

Luke paused, looking at Adam, then at Ruth.

'What do you think happened next?'

'Maybe they all made friends and still lived happily ever after!' Ruth answered.

Adam answered thoughtfully, 'But if it's a true story, that isn't what would have happened. The older brother would be cross because he will think it's unfair. He might be unhappy to see his brother.'

'You are correct, Adam. The older brother was furious because he did as his father asked. He said, "I have worked day and night for you, and you have never even given me a small party with my friends. But your son returns after swallowing up your property, and you give him a huge party."'

'He says "your son", not "my brother". He is very angry,' Adam commented.

'But, Luke,' Ruth asked, 'what did his dad say?'

Luke replied, 'He said, "My son, you are with me

always and all I have is yours. But it was right we should celebrate, because it is as if your brother was dead and now, he is alive, he was lost and is found."'

'That can't be the end! No way!' Ruth pulled a face.

'It is the end. You have to make up your mind about who was right and what the story is about,' Luke shrugged. 'What do you think?'

'Perhaps they have a big fight? That would be a more exciting ending,' Ruth answered.

'Maybe,' Adam rubbed his chin in concentration, 'but is this story really about the sons or about how much the father loved them both?'

'Well, the thing with Jesus is his stories are like puzzles and we have to work out what they mean and what they say to us in our hearts,' Luke smiled. 'So if it's making you ask questions, perhaps I've done a good job at telling the story? Let me write it down now before I forget exactly what I've said.'

'Perhaps you could call the story "The forgiving father"?' Adam suggested.

Luke nodded, spreading out the papyrus and mixing the dish of soot black powder with liquid to make ink. The children got up to leave and he waved goodbye as he dipped his reed pen into the liquid, ready to write.

'We should find Dad,' Adam sighed. 'Can you see the footprints to guide us back?'

Ruth pointed at them in the grass.

'Do you think that the brothers were ever friends again?' Ruth wondered as they walked back.

'I'm not sure,' Adam admitted.

'Let's go and tell Dad the story and see what he thinks,' Ruth suggested. 'Do you think that Luke was a carnival storyteller?'

'I'm not sure,' Adam admitted. 'It feels like his story has got inside me somehow, like it's in my heart, not just in my ears. Does that sound funny?'

THE FORGIVING FATHER

'A bit, but I think I know what you mean,' Ruth nodded.

'I think this is how I would like the story to end, with the brothers making friends.' Ruth showed her picture to Adam. 'It wasn't just a story. It's made me think things, like it's easy to say sorry, but harder to mean it.'

'Yes, I think your picture shows that sorry is something you do, not just something you say,' Adam agreed.

> You can step into this story in Luke's Gospel (Luke 15:11–32).
>
> The story Luke tells Ruth and Adam is one of the most famous stories from the Gospel of Luke. It is often called the parable of the prodigal son. A parable is a short story that points to a lesson about human behaviour. Jesus uses parables as part of his teaching. Jesus uses this story to change people's ideas about God and show that God loves people and forgives them like a caring father. The father, like God, is waiting for his son to return, and when he does, the

boy is welcomed with open arms. However, the second part of the story goes on to show how difficult forgiveness can be for people. The brother finds it much harder to welcome his brother, wanting justice rather than forgiveness.

- **Which of the brothers changes the most in the story?**
What might happen next in the story?
What does the story say to you about God as a loving Father? What does the story say to you about forgiveness?

10
Tongues of Fire
Acts 2:1–13

Nonna Anita hurried Bea and Sandy down the street.

'Quickly, Beatrice and Alessandro, we will be late. The Pantheon will be so busy today!'

'She must be stressed. She is using our Sunday names!' Sandy laughed, knowing his grandmother only called him Alessandro when she felt under pressure.

Bea smiled back.

'Well, we would have been ready earlier if she hadn't decided to give us a history lesson before we set off.' She pretended to speak with her grandmother's Italian accent, 'The Pantheon was built in the reign of Augustus, rebuilt by Emperor Hadrian and has been a Catholic church since – oh, I've already forgotten!' She shook her head.

'Pronto!' Nonna Anita pulled Sandy and Bea before her. 'Quick march!'

Feeling warm and out of breath, they arrived in the piazza, where a queue had formed at the entrance to the vast, round building that dominated the space.

'Woah! The Pantheon really is a Roman building.' Sandy sounded impressed.

'Look at the columns, how many are there? Is the whole building the same age?' Bea replied.

'So now you want a history lesson?' Nonna Anita threw up her arms. 'Later. Let's get in line so we can see the flames.'

'I thought we were going to Mass, Nonna, not a fire show! I'm wearing fancy clothes.' Sandy gestured at his buttoned shirt and trousers. He preferred to be in shorts, but Nonna said he and Beatrice needed to dress respectfully because they were going to church for a feast day.

Nonna Anita nodded. 'You will see. Come, inside.'

Entering the church, Bea and Sandy dipped their fingers in holy water and copied their grandmother, who traced the sign of the cross from forehead to heart, then shoulder to shoulder.

Bea and Sandy gazed around the ancient church as they sat down, waiting for Mass to begin. The church was round with no windows. The light streamed in from a hole at the centre of a massive domed roof that stretched above their heads.

'Wow, Nonna, this place is amazing!' Sandy whispered.

'At the end of Mass, you will be more impressed,' Nonna whispered back, before joining in the opening hymn.

At the end of Mass, as everyone sang the final hymn, Nonna Anita pointed up towards the hole in the roof. What looked like tiny flickers of flame started to fall through the hole, followed by more and more until the whole space of the dome seemed to be alight with fingers of fire. Nonna held out her hand to catch one.

'Look, they are rose petals, like the fire of the Holy Spirit that filled the hearts of the disciples on Pentecost day.'

Bea and Sandy caught petals as they fell. Soon, the floor was carpeted red, and the church smelled of roses. They copied other children, picking up handfuls of petals and scattering them across each other's heads, laughing.

'Gelato time?' Nonna Anita asked.

'Chocolate for me, please,' Bea replied.

'Shall we wait for you here?' Sandy suggested, knowing he wanted to spend a little longer looking at the building. 'I bet there's a long queue.'

Their grandmother agreed but gave them strict instructions not to leave the church until she returned.

Sandy started to walk towards one of the statues when Bea said, 'I'm not sure I understand about the Holy Spirit and the Pentecost word Nonna used. I think I'm going to follow these golden footprints and see if I can find someone to help.'

Her brother turned to tell her to wait but realised his

only choice was to follow as Bea sped off, her grandmother's instruction forgotten.

'Bea, we were supposed to wait inside!' Sandy touched his sister's shoulder as he caught up.

'We are only just outside, and we can follow the footprints back.'

However, as Bea looked around, she realised they were not in the piazza they had walked through earlier that morning. The gigantic columns marking the entrance to the church were not there, and the building behind them looked somehow different.

'Maybe we got turned around and came out of a different door?' Bea turned to Sandy.

'I'm not so sure,' Sandy replied. 'This looks like we are back in Ancient Rome. Look at the clothes the people are wearing.' He pointed as a man walked past, wrapped in a toga, staring at them. 'Let's find our way back.'

But the footprints no longer led inside; instead, they stopped by a man staring up at the building.

'Did you know,' he said as they approached him, 'that the tops of the columns in this temple are made of bronze.' He turned to smile at them. 'You two look lost.'

Bea noticed that the man also wore clothes from a history book, sandals on his feet, a long robe and a cloak around his upper body. He had dark curly hair and a short black beard. The dark brown skin of his forehead creased as he spoke again.

'And you look like your head is on fire.' He pointed at Sandy, whose hair was still full of rose petals.

'Do you know, a few years ago, I had returned to Jerusalem for Shavuot when—'

'What's Shavuot?' Bea interrupted.

'I'm sorry, that was not a good start to my story! Let me explain. I am Jewish, I was born in Jerusalem, but my family buy and sell wine, so I travel a lot. A few years ago, I had made it home in time for our festival of Shavuot, where we celebrate the first harvest of wheat and remember how God revealed himself to us after we fled enslavement in Egypt many centuries ago.

'Jerusalem was very busy, filled with people from all over the world who had come to celebrate the festival. I was heading towards the temple when I heard a noise, like powerful wind, but it wasn't windy.

'I rushed towards the sound, wondering what had happened, and so did everyone else. I was soon jostling

TONGUES OF FIRE

for space as I ran and found myself in a crowd listening to a group of people.'

'Had they made the sound?' asked Sandy.

'No, but they had a strange explanation. They said that they had gathered in a room for the day of celebration when they too had heard a noise like a great wind from heaven. Then they felt filled with a sudden desire to speak about Jesus of Nazareth to the whole city. One of them said it was as if a great fire had been lit inside the room and each of them had been set alight because their hearts burned within them to speak about Jesus.'

Bea shook her head. 'I'm not sure I understand, were they really on fire?'

'I'm not sure,' the man continued. 'I think perhaps they were using picture words to explain how they had been changed by a new Spirit.'

'Oh, so they were comparing it, like when you say someone has a heart of gold to mean they are kind,' Bea said.

The man nodded. 'Or maybe they really saw tongues of fire, I don't know. But what was strange to everyone in the crowd was that they could understand the story that the people were shouting about. Remember, I said there were people who had travelled from far away, from Egypt, Libya and Mesopotamia, as well as many people from Rome. They could all understand them even though they did not speak the same language. What do you think everyone made of that?'

'I guess people thought there was something wrong with them?' Sandy suggested.

'Well, many people thought they were drunk and told them so, but one of them, a man called Peter, spoke to the whole crowd. He said they were not drunk! It was early in the morning! No, it was the Lord God who had poured out his Spirit on them so people of all nations could understand what they said.

TONGUES OF FIRE

'Peter told us all about Jesus, that even though he had been crucified, he had been raised to life. I followed Peter along with others in the crowd and he told us the story of Jesus Christ. He described the miracles Jesus had performed and explained how they were signs of who he really was, not just a prophet but the love of God poured out in human form. Something inside me changed and I felt a great love for Jesus, as though my heart was burning, and I became a follower of Jesus, filled with the Holy Spirit. Now, as I travel, I tell his story so others can learn about his life and teachings.'

'Your heart was set on fire!' Bea exclaimed. 'Like the disciples gathered in the room.'

'That's right!' the man laughed. 'Perhaps one day we will meet as Christ's followers when we gather to pray, share the stories of Jesus and break bread.'

'We know a little about Jesus,' Sandy began. 'We were at Mass with our grandmother, but we have lost her.'

The man smiled. 'I must find my friends and you must go home.'

He pointed at the footprints, which led back towards the building. Bea and Sandy turned to look, and when they turned back, the man had gone. Sandy stepped on the footprints.

'Did that sound like Nonna shouting our names?'

The footprints took them back to the great columns at the church's entrance. Bea picked up a rose petal from the floor and placed it on her forehead.

'Look, it's like the flame of the Holy Spirit in the story.'

'Yes,' said the familiar voice of Nonna Anita behind her. 'And the disciples welcomed the flame of the Holy Spirit into their hearts.'

Bea turned and wrapped her arms around her grandmother.

'Hey, be careful, do you want to wear this gelato as a hat?' she laughed, passing the gelato cone to Bea, the chocolate already down the sides. 'Eat it quickly, it's sticky!'

'Do you want me to take those petals out of your hair?' she asked Sandy as she passed him a tub of gelato.

'No thanks. I think I want to be reminded of the story of the Holy Spirit today. I can tell Dad all about it when we get home.'

'Nonna Anita,' asked Bea, 'is Pentecost day celebrated because it is the day when the Holy Spirit changed the disciples' hearts so they could start telling everyone about Jesus?'

TONGUES OF FIRE

'Bravo! You have listened well, Beatrice!' Nonna replied.

'Well, someone shared a story.' Bea smiled at Sandy as her chocolate gelato ran down her fingers. 'They said the disciples received gifts from the Holy Spirit and shared the story of Jesus to change the world.'

> You can step into this story in the Acts of the Apostles (Acts 2:1–13).
>
> The Acts tell the story of the first followers of Jesus Christ and the Christian community.
>
> Pentecost day in the Acts of the Apostles takes place at the time of the Jewish festival of Shavuot. Jerusalem was busy with people celebrating the two-day festival which marks the first harvest and the gift of the Law to the prophet Moses on Mount Sinai. The word Pentecost means 'fifty', and for Christians, the feast marks fifty days since Easter Sunday. It is the day when the gift of the Holy Spirit is given to Jesus' apostles, which changes them from a group of

people unsure what to do next to the disciples who would announce the good news about Jesus to the world.

> In the story, the Holy Spirit is described as a strong wind and like flames of fire. Why do you think the writer uses picture language to describe the Holy Spirit?
> How does the Holy Spirit change the disciples?
> What do you think is good news about Jesus?

Coming Soon...